Get Well Soon!

I Have an Ear Infection

Gillian Gosman

PowerKiDS
press
New York

Published in 2013 by The Rosen Publishing Group, Inc.
29 East 21st Street, New York, NY 10010

First Edition

Editor: Jennifer Way
Book Design: Greg Tucker
Layout Design: Kate Laczynski

Photo Credits: Cover, pp. 14–15 LWA/Dann Tardif/Blend Images/Getty Images; pp. 4–5 Goodluz/Shutterstock.com; p. 6 Anita Potter/Shutterstock.com; p. 7 (left) Jupiterimages/Brand X Pictures/Thinkstock; p. 7 (right) Jupiterimages/Comstock/Thinkstock; p. 8 Digital Vision/Getty Images; p. 9 Dmitry Naumov/Shutterstock.com; p. 10 Stem Jems/Photo Researchers/Getty Images; p. 11 3445128471/Shutterstock.com; p. 12 iStockphoto/Thinkstock; p. 13 loriklaszlo/Shutterstock.com; p. 16 Alexander Raths/Shutterstock.com; p. 17 CSKN/Shutterstock.com; p. 18 Comstock/Thinkstock; p. 19 Stockbyte/Thinkstock; p. 20 Christopher Robbins/Digital Vision/Thinkstock; p. 21 Wavebreak Media/Thinkstock; p. 22 Brand X Pictures/Thinkstock.

Library of Congress Cataloging-in-Publication Data

Gosman, Gillian.
I have an ear infection / by Gillian Gosman. — 1st ed.
    p. cm. — (Get well soon!)
Includes bibliographical references and index.
ISBN 978-1-4488-7413-2 (library binding)
1. Otitis media in children—Juvenile literature. I. Title.
RF225.G67 2013
618.92'09784—dc23

                    2011051401

Manufactured in the United States of America

CPSIA Compliance Information: Batch #SW12PK: For Further Information contact Rosen Publishing, New York, New York at 1-800-237-9932

Contents

I Have an Ear Infection

Have you been fighting a cold lately? Did your parents and older sisters and brothers have a lot of ear **infections** when they were kids? If you answered yes to any of these questions, you are more likely to get an ear infection.

If you have ever had an ear infection, you would know it! Your ears will hurt. You may feel sick to your stomach. You may have trouble sleeping. An ear infection probably will not last long, though. This book will explain what an ear infection is and how to treat it.

Most kids will have a few ear infections in their lives. Ear infections hurt, but they are usually easily treated. ▶

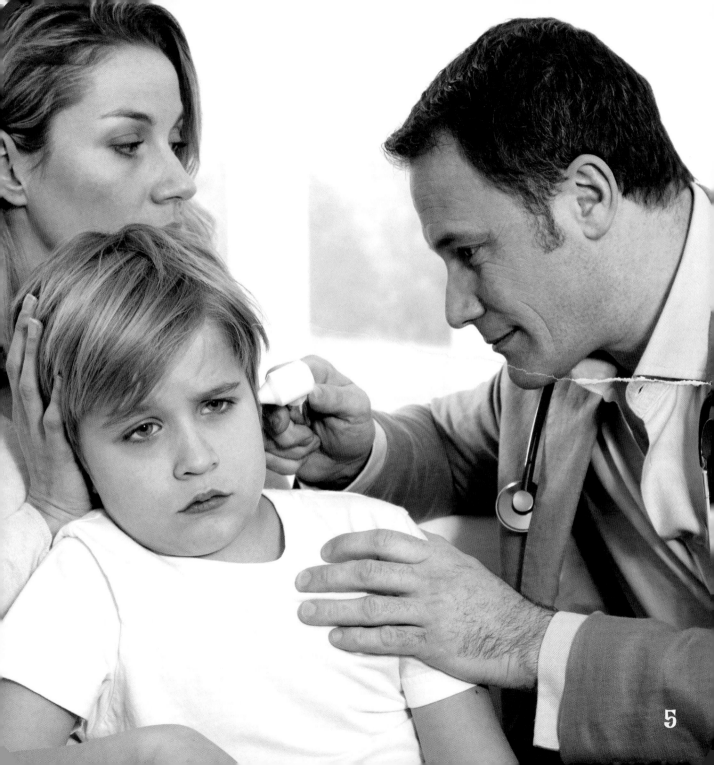
5

What Is an Ear Infection?

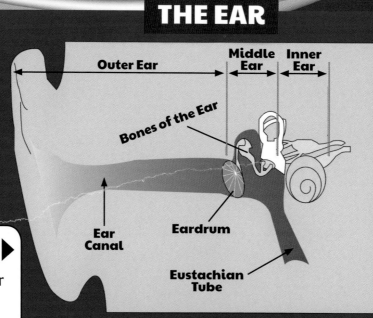

Outer Ear — Middle Ear — Inner Ear

Bones of the Ear

Ear Canal

Eardrum

Eustachian Tube

This diagram shows the parts of your ear. When you have an ear infection, it is likely your middle ear that is infected.

An ear infection is a **bacterial** infection of the ear. The most common kind of ear infection is an infection of the middle ear. The middle ear is connected to the nose and throat by the **Eustachian tube**. The Eustachian tube helps air flow in and

Have you ever had an earache after swimming? That is swimmer's ear, an infection of the outer ear. ▼

When you yawn, you may ▲ sometimes feel a popping in your ears. That is your Eustachian tubes letting air flow into and out of your ears.

out of the middle ear. It also helps **mucus** drain from the middle ear.

Your Eustachian tubes can become swollen, or bigger. When this happens, they cannot drain mucus quickly and completely. The mucus can trap bacteria, and the bacteria then infect the middle ear.

What Causes an Ear Infection?

You are more likely to get an ear infection when your allergies are acting up. ▼

The Eustachian tubes may become swollen for many reasons. If you have a cold or **allergies**, your Eustachian tubes may become **irritated**. Babies' and children's Eustachian tubes are shorter than adults and get infected more easily. This is why ear infections are more common in kids than in adults.

Very young children who are getting their first teeth have more

The process of teething can irritate the Eustachian tubes and lead to an ear infection.
▼

mucus and saliva in their mouths. This can make it more likely for them to get ear infections. Smoke or other things in the air around you can also irritate your Eustachian tubes and lead to ear infections.

9

What's Going On in My Body?

Bacteria are tiny living things. They live well in wet, dark places. They do best in the body of a host, or another living thing. When bacteria enter the body, they can easily spread and multiply, or make copies of themselves. The body's **immune system** makes the body a bad place for the bacteria to live. For

▲

White blood cells (white circles) are part of your body's immune system. They fight infections. These cells travel in your bloodstream with red blood cells (red circles).

example, the immune system raises the body's temperature and sends germ-fighting cells to battle the bacteria. A lot of the body's energy is used to fight the infection, which is why we usually feel tired when we are sick.

When you have an ear infection, your ears may ▶ hurt and feel stuffed up.

How Did I Get an Ear Infection?

Ear infections are more common during the winter because colds and other illnesses are more common in the winter. ▼

An ear infection is not a **contagious** illness. That means that it is not caught through contact with a sick person. However, ear infections are most common when colds and other contagious infections are in the air.

The common cold **virus** travels through the air in tiny drops of mucus that leave the body through a sick person's nose and mouth when he coughs, sneezes, or blows his nose. This mucus can then make its way into the noses, eyes, and mouths of healthy people and make them sick. They may get a cold and then an ear infection.

When you have a cold, the mucus can get into your Eustachian tubes. This can cause an ear infection.

Going to the Doctor

If you think you might have an ear infection, you should visit the doctor. The doctor will ask you questions about how you feel. She might also ask the adult who comes with you questions about your family history. This is because ear infections are more common in children whose parents, sisters, and brothers also had ear infections.

The doctor will examine, or look at, your ear using an instrument called an **otoscope**. An otoscope is like a flashlight but with a small, bright tip.

> The doctor will look into your ears. This will tell her how bad your ear infection is so she can decide how to treat your illness. ▶

Signs and Symptoms

This is an otoscope. It lets the doctor see into your middle ear and look for signs of an ear infection.
▼

When you visit the doctor, she will gather information by examining you and doing tests. The pieces of information the doctor gathers about an illness are called signs. Using an otoscope, the doctor might see redness and bloody mucus in your ear.

◀ Ear pain is a symptom of an ear infection.

The patient also describes the illness to the doctor. The pieces of information the patient gives the doctor are called symptoms. Symptoms of an ear infection include ear pain, **vomiting**, **diarrhea**, fever, and some hearing loss in the infected ear.

17

How an Ear Infection Is Treated

Kids who have lots of ear infections may need to have tubes placed in their ears. It is a fast, simple operation. Most patients are back at school in a day or so.

▼

An infection of the middle ear can go away without medical treatment. Often a doctor will **prescribe** a medicine called an **antibiotic**, though. Patients take antibiotics twice each day for 10 days. Usually the bacteria have been killed by then, and the patient will feel much better.

Antibiotic eardrops are the most common treatment for ear infections. ▼

If a patient has many ear infections, though, the doctor may tell him to take antibiotics every day for a longer period of time. If the ear infections continue, the doctor may think the next step should be placing tiny tubes in the ear to help empty the middle ear of mucus.

How to Prevent an Ear Infection

Washing your hands often is a good way to prevent colds and other illnesses. Therefore, it is a good way to keep from getting ear infections. ▼

The best way to prevent ear infections is to avoid the things that cause them. Try not to spend a lot of time with people sick with colds. If you do, wash your hands often to kill any germs you have picked up. Avoid smoke and things you are allergic to. This will help keep your Eustachian tubes from becoming irritated.

It is important to take all of your medicine as directed. You should follow any other instructions your doctor gives, too. ▶

A way to prevent getting another ear infection is to treat today's ear infection well. Take all of the antibiotic medicine prescribed by your doctor, even if you begin to feel better before the medicine is finished.

21

The Road to Recovery

Most patients begin feeling better one or two days after beginning to take an antibiotic medicine. Sometimes, an ear infection can cause the **eardrum** to rupture, or break. A tear or hole in the eardrum usually heals on its own in one or two months.

An ear infection usually clears up in a few days. Then you will be ready to get back to your regular activities.

It is very important to visit your doctor, follow your treatment plan, and take care of yourself. This will put you on the road to recovery and to feeling better.

Glossary

allergies (A-lur-jeez) Bad reactions to certain things, such as animals or pollen.

antibiotic (an-tee-by-AH-tik) Something that kills bacteria.

bacterial (bak-TIR-ee-ul) Caused by bacteria, the tiny living things that cannot be seen with the eye alone. Some bacteria cause illness or rotting, but others are helpful.

contagious (kun-TAY-jus) Can be passed on.

diarrhea (dy-uh-REE-uh) Having very watery stools and having to go very often.

eardrum (EER-drum) A thin sheet of skin inside the ear that shakes when sound enters the ear.

Eustachian tube (yoo-STAY-shun TOOB) The tube that connects the middle ear to the nose and throat.

immune system (ih-MYOON SIS-tem) The system that keeps the body safe from sicknesses.

infections (in-FEK-shunz) Sicknesses caused by germs.

irritated (IR-uh-tayt-ed) Having pain or discomfort.

mucus (MYOO-kus) Thick, slimy matter produced by the body.

otoscope (OH-tuh-skohp) A tool used by a doctor to look into a patient's ears.

prescribe (prih-SKRYB) To order a certain kind of medicine.

virus (VY-rus) Something tiny that causes a disease.

vomiting (VO-mut-ing) When the stomach pushes its contents up through to the mouth when one is sick.

Index

Websites

Due to the changing nature of Internet links, PowerKids Press has developed an online list of websites related to the subject of this book. This site is updated regularly. Please use this link to access the list: www.powerkidslinks.com/gws/ear/